CONTENTS

❊ I ❊

THE QUEEN OF EGYPT

I will not be triumphed over.
   Cleopatra

❧

Everybody knows her name: Cleopatra, the last queen of Egypt. She was exotic and seductive, a femme fatale who caused the downfall of Julius Caesar and Mark Antony alike. She was beautiful. She was power-hungry. She committed suicide by reptile and died as dramatically as she lived. Her name is synonymous with sex.

❧

That's what everybody knows. Is there anything else about her that remains to be learned?

In short, the answer is yes.

A QUEEN IS BORN

❦

In 69 BC, a little girl was born in Alexandria. She was
named Cleopatra VII Thea Philopater, which means
"She Who Loves Her Father". The name Cleopatra was
one that Ptolemy had brought with him from Macedonia. It
was the name of Alexander the Great's own sister, and of
many ladies in the royal line of Macedonia. None of those
women would ever hope to equal the most famous Cleopatra
of them all, though, the last royal Cleopatra in the world.

❦

SHE WAS BORN into a world of conflict and corruption. Her
grandfather, Ptolemy XI, had left the kingdom of Egypt to
Rome in his will. When Ptolemy XII Auletus assumed the
throne, Rome allowed it, mostly because the Senate was
concerned with domestic business and didn't want to be trou-
bled with the effort and expense it would take to set up shop
in a foreign colony. It's important to remember this fact,

because from this moment forward, many in Rome considered Egypt to be their possession. This would come into play in the future in very dramatic and violent ways.

⚜

PTOLEMY XII AULETUS was married to two women. One was his niece and cousin, Cleopatra V. He was also married to a woman named Cleopatra Tryphaena, who may or may not have been Cleopatra VII Thea Philopater's mother, and who may or may not have been Ptolemy's sister, as well. The writings are obscure and confusing on this point, and it may well have been that Cleopatra V and Cleopatra VI are one and the same. In truth, nobody really knows.

⚜

CLEOPATRA VII'S mother is not truly known. She could have been the product of the usual Ptolemaic incest, or she might have been born to a third queen that history does not record. Certainly, it was not unheard of for pharaohs of Egypt to have more than one wife; Ramesses II was the most-married pharaoh in history, with seven queens and over one hundred and fifty concubines. Some people claim that her mother was black African, but while the court at Alexandria was certainly cosmopolitan, the royal family itself was careful to maintain its Macedonian heritage. No matter who her mother actually was, we can say with certainty that Cleopatra VII Thea Philopater was of Greek descent.

⚜

SHE WAS the second of Ptolemy XIII Auletus's children. Her older sister, Berenike IV, had been born in Alexandria in 77

4

BC, probably to Auletus and his sister Cleopatra V Tryphaena. Cleopatra VII Thea Philopater was next in 69 BC, then three more children in close succession: Arsinoe IV (born in 65 BC), Ptolemy XIII Philopater (born in 61 BC) and Ptolemy XIV (born in 59 BC).

⚜

THE ROYAL CHILDREN were raised in Alexandria with the best of everything, as one might expect. Ptolemy XII Auletus had, despite a series of failed harvests, added to the coffers of Egypt through direct trade with India and with the horn of Africa. From these distant sources, the Egyptians imported spices, slaves, resins, gems, perfumes, silks and other fineries that the Egyptians then sold to the civilizations of the Mediterranean, specifically Rome and Greece. It was this fabulous wealth that once again attracted the attention of the Romans.

ROME COMES TO EGYPT

༄

Ptolemy XII Auletes, like many of the Ptolemies
before him, knew that the security of his realm
depended upon the continued support of Rome. His
enthusiasm for the protection of this increasingly-powerful
neighbor was tempered by concern that one day Rome
might come to take what it had been given in Ptolemy
X's will.

༄

IN 64 BC, Pompey the Great, who was a member of the
First Triumvirate along with Crassus and Julius Caesar,
marched into the Syrian territory of Egypt's old enemies, the
Seleucids, and took their country away. Pragmatically, Auletes
sent a handful of cavalry soldiers to "assist" Pompey in this
endeavor, and upon the Romans' victory, the Egyptian king
threw a lavish celebratory banquet. It didn't matter that
Pompey was too busy elsewhere to attend the party in

Alexandria; Auletes made certain that the Romans knew that he was their man.

☙❧

THE CONSTANT WARS of the Ptolemies had taken a toll on the country, and Auletes had spent far too much money that he really didn't have to celebrate Pompey. Worse, the Romans had yet to recognize him as the legitimate ruler of Egypt after all of the turmoil. The late Ptolemy XI had been their chosen client king, and they were still put out by the way he had been removed from the scene.

☙❧

CLEOPATRA, living in her father's house, would have been aware of the strength of Rome and the necessity of courting that distant city's favor. She would have heard the names of the Triumvirate, and as a true princess of the Ptolemies, she must have found Roman power intriguing. She was a child of marked intellect. Watching the lengths that Auletes was willing to go to in order to secure Roman approval must have been instructive as well as humiliating. Instructive, because she learned how to curry favor and how to wield it once it was obtained. Humiliating, because in the eyes of Egypt, the king and royal family were gods, and here was a god beseeching approval from mere mortals. It was an offense to the very divinity of the pharaoh. Cleopatra never, ever forgot that she was a goddess.

☙❧

IN 59, when Cleopatra was ten years old, Rome at last began to show some warming toward Auletes. Julius Caesar agreed

to argue on his behalf before the Roman Senate and promote him as the proper client king in Alexandria for the low, low price of six thousand talents – the entire revenue of Egypt for six months. Auletes was happy to pay. Caesar, as consul, shared his bribe with his old friend and rival Pompey, and the two of them together succeeded in having the Senate recognize Auletes as a friend and ally of Rome.

⚜

THERE WAS a price to be paid, of course. Auletes' brother, also named Ptolemy, had taken the throne of Cyprus, but he had neglected to gain the approval and recognition of Rome. The Roman general Cato the Younger was given the job of taking Cyprus back by force. Although his brother was imperiled and he was technically losing land, Auletes kept silent about the attack by his Roman masters, which infuriated the volatile people of Alexandria. When Ptolemy of Cyprus committed suicide to escape the shame of his defeat, the people of Alexandria broke out into riots.

⚜

AULETES GATHERED what riches he could grab and ran to Rhodes, leaving his family behind. The people of Alexandria declared that Cleopatra Tryphaena and Berenike IV, Aulete's wife and daughter, respectively, would thereafter share the throne. They began to ferret out the corruption that had set in with Auletes' tax collectors, a move that relieved an intolerable financial burden for the common Egyptian and also won the loyalty of those commoners to the two queens.

ONE QUEEN ON THE THRONE

※

Cleopatra Tryphaena died not long after the two women ascended to the throne, and Berenike IV became the sole queen. There were efforts to find her a husband, and one man actually succeeded in marrying her, but he was strangled immediately after the wedding ceremony on the queen's orders. She finally married Archelaos, the son of a general who had served King Mithridates of Pontus, his lack of royal blood offset by his supposed military acumen. Alexandria was in turmoil, and the reign of the Ptolemies was insecure.

※

AULETES RAN TO CATO, who was at that time preparing to take over the government of Cyprus. He begged for military assistance in taking back his capital city, but Cato rebuffed him and told him to go back to Egypt. Auletes instead went to Rome, where he found shelter in the home of Pompey the

Great. He went to the Senate and implored them for aid in returning him to power, but the Senate was in no mood to help him. Rome had itself just struggled out of one civil war following the overthrow of the dictator Sulla and was lurching toward a new one, and there was no appetite in the Senate for fighting on foreign soil.

⚜

AULETES FLED to the Temple of Artemis in Ephesus, where he went into hiding. In Rome, Pompey continued to harangue the Senate on the pharaoh's behalf, but he met with no success. Auletes then resorted to the Roman governor of Syria, which had only recently become a Roman province. The governor's name was Aulus Gabinius, and he was receptive to Auletes' cause after a suitable application of coin.

⚜

GABINIUS WAS the commander of a fighting force made up of soldiers from Gaul and Germany, and they were loyal to the paymaster if not to their commander. The Roman force, in support of Auletes for as long as he was paying, invaded Egypt and easily took the Delta city of Pelusium. Berenike IV sent her husband Archelaos to head off the invasion and became a widow. The Egyptian forces were decimated, and with Roman forces at his back – led by a notable young cavalry officer named Marcus Antonius, known to history as Mark Antony - Auletes returned to Alexandria. His first order of business was to murder the queen, his own daughter.

⚜

DURING ALL OF THIS TURMOIL, Cleopatra was living in

Alexandria, developing a taste for the power that her older sister held. When Auletes was returned to the throne, Cleopatra was his oldest surviving child, and he must have recognized the naked ambition in her, for he made it known that he preferred to be succeeded by his oldest son, Ptolemy XIII, who was actually the third of his remaining children.

⚜

CLEOPATRA GREW up speaking Greek and a number of other languages; indeed, the great Roman historian Plutarch credited her with the ability to speak in many tongues. Unlike most of her dynasty, Cleopatra also endeavored to speak Egyptian with absolute fluency, and so understood Egyptian history and the complex religion of her country. She was exhaustively well tutored in everything from history to astronomy to medicine and toxicology. Her interest in medicine and poison sprang from the plagues that swept through Egypt in her childhood, and the belief that plague was caused by poisonous miasma. She was also studying poison as a potential assassination/execution method.

⚜

SHE BEGAN to present herself as the living embodiment of the goddess Isis, laying claim to the divinity that had cloaked the pharaohs of years past. She personally oversaw the investiture of the new sacred Buchis bull, and her pious observations of Egyptian religion won her many adherents. She was popular with the Egyptian people but less so with the Greeks of Alexandria, who had been convinced by Pothinus and his cronies that she was snubbing them. This is something that would come into play in later years.

❦

AULETES FELL ill and vanished from the public eye, and while he was ailing, Cleopatra had herself named coregent. In truth, he was probably already dead, and most likely through unnatural means. Once the new queen's grasp on power was consolidated, the demise of the pharaoh was made known. Cleopatra was eighteen years old and the Queen of Egypt at last.

❦ II ❦

SIBLING RIVALRY

My honour was not yielded, but conquered merely.
   Cleopatra

❦

Unfortunately for Cleopatra's ambition, Aulete's will had made its way to Pompey the Great, who was named its executor. The document proved that the dead king's wish was to have Cleopatra and Ptolemy XIII, then ten years old, as co-rulers upon the Horus Throne. The young prince's regent, the eunuch Pothinus, and two guardians, the general Achillas and a mathematician named Theodotus of Chios, seized this opportunity to bring themselves into power. With Pompey and Gabinius behind them, they were able to compel the young queen to accept her brother as husband and co-regent.

❦

It was abundantly clear to anyone who knew her (or who had known any of her forebears) that Cleopatra had no wish to be saddled with her brother, especially since his installation as co-regent severely diminished her own power, pushing her back into the role of helper and supporter that Egyptian queens were expected to play. She gathered supporters to herself, and she watched for an opportunity to discredit her brother and his keepers.

※

The opportunity came in the form of a failed harvest. Grain, which normally was so plentiful in Egypt, was becoming hard to come by, and in Ptolemy XIII's name, an edict was sent out telling the people to send all of their excess grain to Alexandria on pain of death. The people of Egypt's hinterlands roared in anger, and Cleopatra tried to make the debacle seem to be the fault of her brother's regent, Pothinus. The people of Alexandria, though, had profited from the situation, and they supported Pothinus and Ptolemy, the authors of their salvation from hunger. Cleopatra was obliged to leave the capital and go to Syria-Palestine, where she set up her own capital at Ashkelon and went to work building an army.

POMPEY THE GREAT ARRIVES
IN EGYPT

☙❧

A chillas, Ptolemy's military advisor, took the boy with him at the head of the army and traveled to the Delta to wait for Cleopatra to return with her forces. When an army appeared on the horizon, though, it was not the queen returning to wage civil war. Rather, it was the forces of Pompey, the self-proclaimed patron of the Ptolemies.

☙❧

POMPEY HAD RECENTLY FALLEN on hard times. His war with Julius Caesar had been going badly, and his army had been crushed in Greece. His flight in search of sanctuary brought him to Egypt, where he supposed he would find warm welcome, considering all he had done to secure the throne for Auletes. Pompey's luck had run out.

☙❧

CAESAR WAS a vigorous and successful general, fresh from his victories over the Britons and the Celts, and he had brought such riches back to Rome from his conquest of Gaul that he was well loved by the common folk. He was also a canny and talented soldier, and after Pompey's disaster at the Battle of Pharsalus, it was clear that when the Roman civil war ended, Caesar would be victorious.

۞

ACHILLAS AND POTHINUS wanted to avoid Caesar's wrath, which they were certain would fall upon them if they protected Pompey. They also fancied that they might gain a substantial monetary reward from the victorious Roman if they helped him with his Pompey problem. When Pompey came to Ptolemy for asylum, he was instead met by the soldiers of Gabinius. One of the men who had been assigned by Gabinius to the Egyptian king's army had actually served under Pompey, he stabbed Pompey to death while the general's wife and children looked on in horror. Pothinus had Pompey's head removed and preserved as a present for Caesar, who was expected to arrive at any time, since he had been in hot pursuit of his rival. The gift was made in Ptolemy's name.

۞

THERE COULD HAVE BEEN few worse decisions. Contrary to expectation, Caesar was devastated by his rival's death, both because they had been close friends for decades and because he had wanted to offer Pompey amnesty, a politically shrewd maneuver that would win him friends in Rome. Instead, he was left with Pompey's head in literally in his hands. He took

the horrid object and kept it in safe keeping until he could give his old friend a proper burial.

WORD OF CAESAR'S presence in Egypt reached Cleopatra in Ashkelon, and she sent him a missive describing her predicament and begging him for his assistance. The Roman general went at last to Alexandria, where he was greeted with hostility by a citizenry who had heard rumors that he intended to depose Ptolemy and take Egypt for himself. He deftly deflected those rumors by settling into guest quarters at the palace and letting it be known that his only purpose in coming to Alexandria was to ensure that Auletes' will would be honored.

MAKING AN ENTRANCE

※

Cleopatra desperately wanted to plead her case to Caesar in person, but Alexandria was a dangerous place for her. The antipathy toward her that Ptolemy XIII and his regents had aroused made her exceedingly unpopular, and her brother's keepers had set guards all through the city with orders to murder on sight if she should dare set foot in the capital again.

※

NOW HER FLAIR for the dramatic came into full force in an episode that has become justifiably famous in centuries of art and literature. She left Ashkelon with a small force of retainers, but once she was within close range of Alexandria, she left them behind. The young queen, now twenty-two years old, set sail in a tiny boat, accompanied only by a Sicilian retainer named Apollodorus. Together they sailed into the harbor of Alexandria under the cover of night.

☙❧

ONCE THEY WERE SAFELY on Alexandria's shore, Cleopatra stretched out on a bright carpet, which Apollodorus rolled up around her. He whip-stitched the ends together and carried her to the palace, announcing to the guards that he was delivering a purchase to the Roman visitor. Caesar had been receiving supplies and luggage all day, so the guards thought nothing of it and waved them through.

☙❧

APOLLODORUS CARRIED his royally-laden carpet into the general's bedroom, where Caesar was sitting and writing. When the door was safely closed and the guards were gone, the courtier cut the stitches and unrolled the carpet, revealing the somewhat disheveled but still stunning young queen to the surprised general.

☙❧

CLEOPATRA IS EVEN NOW RENOWNED for her beauty, and in the day, even her enemy Plutarch spoke almost reverently of her charms. He wrote that

> "interaction with her was captivating, and her appearance, along with her persuasiveness in discussing and her character that accompanied every interchange, was stimulating. Pleasure also came with the tone of her voice; and her tongue was like a many-stringed instrument..."

ROMANS HAD ALWAYS BEEN INTRIGUED by the exotic, and Caesar was no exception. He was already beguiled by the strangeness of Egypt, and now here was her displaced queen, unveiling herself like a bride on her wedding night, young and beautiful and in his power. She exhibited courage as well as beauty, and the boldness of her clandestine trip into the palace was certainly not lost on him. She was also fabulously rich, and Caesar's wars had been expensive in the extreme. It is no surprise that he was attracted to her.

CLEOPATRA, meanwhile, was faced with a man like none she had known before. He was cultured and intelligent, and they shared a love of scholarship. There were more prosaic and physical qualities about him that would have attracted her, too. As Suetonius wrote in *The Divine Julius Caesar*, he was tall and handsome, fair-haired and comely with "dark and lively eyes". He dressed more flamboyantly than Romans normally did, notably wearing a purple-striped tunic and a purple cloak everywhere he went. He wore long sleeves on his tunic in the Greek style, and he wore his belt loosely, again more in keeping with the ways of Alexander than those of Romulus. Caesar was not just attractive, he was also physically powerful and strong, and before the two met, he had earned a reputation as a promiscuous and voracious lover of both genders. One Roman wit called him "every woman's husband and every man's wife". He was also powerful, and to an ambitious woman, power was an aphrodisiac. He was strong enough to defend her from her enemies, and powerful enough that she could trust his patronage to help steady her nascent rule.

☙❦❧

THEY WERE ENAMORED of one another almost instantly, and most believe that they became lovers that very night. Caesar was a great admirer of women and a known philanderer, and with her many charms and graces, the queen was a prize to be won. Cleopatra was impressive enough that by morning, Caesar had issued a proclamation naming her as the rightful co-ruler with Ptolemy XIII. In one eventful and dramatic night, Cleopatra had gone from exile to queen once more.

❧ III ❧

CAESAR AND CLEOPATRA

Fool! Don't you see now that I could have poisoned you a hundred times had I been able to live without you.

    Cleopatra

❧❧❧

When Ptolemy XIII and his retainers found his much-loathed sister in the presence of Caesar, he threw an adolescent tantrum that included throwing his diadem across the room. Pothinus, Theodotus and Achillas were no less displeased. Pothinus and Achillas debated assassinating Cleopatra and Caesar, but they decided not to act on the grounds that it might endanger their meal ticket, the young king, and make him an enemy of Rome. Unfortunately for the two conspirators, Caesar's barber overheard their conversation, and he brought the news to the general. Pothinus was

arrested and killed, and as recompense for the murder of Pompey, he was decapitated, too.

❧

Achillas managed to escape. He met up with an army loyal to Ptolemy XIII that numbered more than 20,000 strong, marching to Alexandria from Pelusium. They came to the capital city and put it under siege.

❧

Inside the city walls, Caesar and Cleopatra had only 4,000 soldiers in the four legions who had accompanied him to Egypt from the battles with Pompey in Greece. They also had Ptolemy XIII, Arsinoe and the youngest prince, Ptolemy XIV, as hostages. Both sides settled down for a long battle of wills.

❧

Caesar summoned reinforcements from Anatolia and the Levant, where he had loyal soldiers, some led by Mark Antony, who had distinguished himself not just in the restoration of Auletes but also in Caesar's conquest of Gaul. Meanwhile, in an effort to protect against an invasion by sea, at Cleopatra's suggestion, Caesar ordered his men to set fire to the Roman triremes, the Egyptian royal fleet and all merchant vessels docked in Alexandria's harbor. The wreckage would prevent Achillas and his men from attacking from the water.

❧

It was a sound plan, if only the weather had been on their side. They succeeded in destroying the ships, but the fire was fanned by the wind and spread to the library at Alexandria. Hundreds of priceless works were lost in that fire, although the library itself was not truly lost until the riots of the early Christian period.

⚜

The smoke and confusion of the burning in the harbor created havoc in the city and in the palace, and Arsinoe, just as crafty and ambitious as her older sister, contrived to escape. She fled Alexandria with her eunuch tutor, Ganymedes, and joined up with Achillas and his army. Once she arrived in their midst, they proclaimed her the true queen of Egypt, in coregency with Ptolemy XIII.

⚜

Cleopatra was beside herself with fury at her sister's escape, but Caesar thought he could use it to his advantage. Given how badly the Ptolemies usually got on with one another, he decided to release Ptolemy XIII to Achillas, believing that the two siblings would start to squabble and thereby break down the cohesion of their faction. He didn't realize that their hatred for Rome and Cleopatra was greater than their hatred for each other. Instead of fighting between themselves, they banded together, and the unified co-regency legitimized their point of view among their soldiers and Macedonian-descended citizens.

⚜

Arsinoe and her tutor had their own ideas about how Achillas

was conducting his siege. When he rejected their suggestions, Arinsoe had him strangled. She replaced him with Ganymedes, who promptly began injecting seawater into the fresh canals that brought potable water to the city of Alexandria. Cleopatra ordered the digging of new wells inside the city limits and managed to stave off disaster.

☙❧

Fortunately for Cleopatra and her general, the Roman reinforcements arrived at Peluisum and marched on Alexandria, breaking the siege. Ptolemy XIII, whom Achillas had forced to ride at the head of his army, now led his troops in fleeing from the city. Caesar and his soldiers pursued them closely, and in the course of a long and brutal battle, Ptolemy XIII drowned in the Nile. Arsinoe was captured, and Cleopatra was finally and definitively named queen. For propriety's sake, she took her youngest brother, Ptolemy XIV, as husband and co-regent, although he had no power to speak of.

☙❧

It was all good news for Caesar and Cleopatra, but their best news was yet to come.

HEIR TO THE THRONE

࿔

During the war with Ptolemy and Arsinoe, later called "the War of the Scepters," Cleopatra learned that she was pregnant with her first child – Caesar's child. The great man had a wife in Rome named Calpurnia, but she had only given him one child, a daughter, Julia. That daughter had in fact married Pompey, but she had died in childbirth, leaving Caesar childless. One can only imagine his great joy at the news.

࿔

FOR CLEOPATRA, it was the opportunity to once again show-case herself as the Living Isis, the mother goddess and queen of the Egyptian pantheon. She dressed like the goddess and had numerous statutes and carvings made of herself in the guise Isis nursing Horus, the sun god, her child and the symbol of the pharaohs for millennia.

※

THE VICTORY over her siblings gave her the chance to bring the people her message that the great goddess had returned to Egypt. With Caesar at her side, playing Roman god to her Egyptian goddess, the queen took 400 Roman ships and her own pleasure barque and spent many months on a waterborne version of the Roman Triumph. The couple visited temples and made appropriate offerings, especially at temples to Isis and the Mammisi, small sacred houses attached to the temples that were set aside as sacred spaces where women could safely give birth. Considering that childbirth was as lethal to women as warfare was to men, it stood to reason that there would have been extra precautions, and Cleopatra wanted the gods on her side when her time came to bring her child into the world.

※

AT SOME POINT in this procession from temple to temple, probably when they reached Memphis, where Cleopatra had a relative serving as high priest, Caesar and Cleopatra were married. The fact that Caesar already had a wife back in Rome mattered little, if at all. Egyptian kings had taken multiple wives in the past, and there was no stigma at all attached to bigamy. Cleopatra continued as co-regent with Ptolemy XIV, but there was no doubt at all that Caesar was Egypt's king.

CAESAR RETURNS TO ROME

❦

T he ceremony was viewed a good deal more harshly back in the Eternal City. As Dr. Joann Fletcher writes, Romans took a dim view of Egypt and the ancient country's ways. Egypt was "the home of everything unacceptable." Roman law did not recognize marriages of Roman citizens to foreigners, and Caesar's friends and enemies never referred to Cleopatra as his wife. She was always his "mistress," and it is this stigma of home-wrecking that has stained her image.

❦

THE SENATE WAS BECOMING impatient with Caesar's long sojourn in Egypt, which had stretched into a stay of two years. They blamed Cleopatra's beguiling temptations and decadent ways for distracting Caesar and keeping him away from his duties, which was only partially true. He was also delayed by the for Alexandria and by the consistently

inclement weather, which made sailing out of the harbor dangerous and unwise.

⚜

EVENTUALLY, the grumbling in the Senate was loud enough that Caesar had to pay attention. Taking Arsinoe with him as his hostage and prisoner, he left Alexandria to travel along the shore of the Mediterranean, traveling through the eastern territories. He left four legions behind in Egypt to protect Cleopatra and their unborn child, and to mark the occasion of his departure, the queen commissioned a massive monument that would become known as the Caesarium.

⚜

CAESAR PAID visits to all of the kings and kingdoms who had supported Ptolemy in his war against Cleopatra, and by dint of numbers and strength, he compelled them to pay reparations and swear allegiance to him and to Rome. Those who would not comply were replaced with more pliant rulers. He encountered Pompey's sons, who attacked him but were repulsed after a grim battle. The sons fled to Spain, and Caesar continued on his way, his reputation bolstered by his victory.

⚜

THINGS AT HOME weren't all cheery, as he discovered. His trusted deputy, Mark Antony, had fallen under the spell of an actress and was comporting himself scandalously, drinking to excess and once even vomiting in the middle of the Forum. He was seen with his actress lover in public places, humiliating his proper patrician wife, and he was often seen driving

around the city in a chariot pulled by lions while he was dressed as Hercules, from whom his family claimed descent. He had also been enriching himself by seizing Ptolemy's assets in the eastern provinces, and when Caesar learned of this, he forced Antony to pay for them at market cost. Antony had also taken Cicero, a vociferous Republican and Pompey supporter, and placed him under house arrest. Caesar intervened and ordered that Cicero should be released, on the condition that he expressed his gratitude with large amounts of coin. This he did, and Cicero went free to complain another day.

SUSPECTING the Antony was becoming a liability, he removed him from his position as his deputy and replaced him with Marcus Aemilius Lepidus. Antony was brokenhearted, not for his loss of power and prestige, although that certainly would have stung; mostly, he was saddened because he had failed Caesar, a man he virtually worshipped. He was able to convince Caesar not to turn from him completely, and he embarked on a program of personal rehabilitation.

MEANWHILE, back in Egypt, Cleopatra gave birth to a healthy baby boy, whom she named Ptolemy Caesar. The child is best known today by his nickname, Caesarion, meaning "little Caesar". He resembled his Roman father, and he was the heir to the throne that Cleopatra had desired. She sent the happy news to Caesar, who received it while he was still en route to Rome. He was overjoyed and told close friends Gaius Matius and Gaius Oppius of his happiness and his intention to create laws that would legitimize his marriage

to multiple women if it was done to ensure an heir. In celebration of their good fortune, he issued coins showing
Cleopatra as Venus, suckling a baby.

CAESAR AND CLEOPATRA WERE HAPPY, but their happiness
was a bone in the throat for the Roman Senate.

EGYPT ON FOREIGN SOIL

౸

When Caesar finally reached Rome, he prepared for his fourth Triumph. A triumph in Rome was a spectacular parade where a victorious general would show his soldiers, the booty he had captured, and votive offerings to the gods. The prize offering would be the ruler or leader of whatever group he had vanquished. After his victory over Gaul and Britain, Caesar had brought back the Celtic warlord Vercingetorix, who was strangled to death on the steps of the Temple of Mars as sacrifice to the god of war.

౸

IN HIS FOURTH TRIUMPH, the spectacle was even flashier than normal, for he had the riches of Egypt to display. Chief among these riches was the young deposed queen Arsinoe, little more than a girl, who was dragged through the Roman streets in a cart, bound in golden chains. She was so beautiful

and looked so young that the people of Rome stirred with sympathy for her, and Caesar, who was rarely tone deaf to popular opinion, opted to display his famous mercy and release her instead of having her strangled, too. She was sent to live in exile at the Temple of Artemis in Ephesus, where her father had once repaired when he, too, had been briefly deposed. She must have seen it as a sort of omen that she was destined to follow in Auletes' footsteps, for she began scheming almost as soon as her feet touched the ground in the sanctuary.

⚜

NOT LONG AFTER THE TRIUMPH, Caesar sent for Cleopatra to join him in Rome. Because Roman law forbade foreign heads of state from residing within the city limits, he put her up in his Greek-style garden estate on the banks of the Tiber River while he himself stayed in the city proper with his long-suffering wife, Calpurnia. He met Cleopatra and little Caesarion at the gate and accorded them the highest of honors, and the people of Rome were agape. They had never seen any woman as bold and colorful as the Egyptian queen. Roman women were supposed to be plain, obedient, and largely housebound. Cleopatra wore cosmetics and gauzy gowns that left little to the imagination. She was constantly a vision of jewels and gold, when Roman matrons were expected to eschew such ornaments.

⚜

SHE STAYED in Rome for two years, frequently appearing in public at Caesar's side, riding through the streets of the suburbs in a litter carried by slaves. She was exotic, beautiful, and one of a kind. She held frequent dinners, inviting the

brightest minds of Rome to come and hold philosophical debates while they ate in a hall that was decorated in colors and styles more suited to Greece than to Rome. Her dinners were something of a local scandal, full of musicians and naked slaves and fodder for rumor mongers. The Republicans in the Senate were horrified by her presence, and by Caesar's "flaunting" of their relationship, but they still fell over one another in pursuit of invitations to sit and be appalled at Cleopatra's table. The queen knew that she was wildly popular among the common people of Rome, like a movie star among the masses today. She was gathering positive public opinion, something that galled the Senators to no end – especially Cicero, who had a special hatred for her and refused to use her name. She knew how to appeal to men and women alike, and soon the ladies of the city were mimicking her clothing, her cosmetics and her way of life.

MARK ANTONY and his wife may have been regulars at Cleopatra's dinners, especially considering that the young warrior and Caesar were intimate friends. Certainly, the young man made no effort to conceal his fascination with the queen. Once, while he was listening to a political speech in the Forum, he noted Cleopatra being carried past in her litter. He abandoned his party and took up position beside her, walking her all the way home to Caesar's villa outside of town. This single-minded admiration was a hint of things to come.

❧ IV ❧

ASSASSINATION

All strange and terrible events are welcome, but comforts we despise.

Cleopatra

❧❧❧

While she had hosted him in Egypt, Cleopatra had shown Caesar what it truly meant to be divine royalty. She had shown him temples and statues, palaces and worshipful crowds. As the Living Isis, she convinced Caesar, descendant of Venus, that he deserved the same sort of treatment. His ego whole-heartedly agreed. When she came to Rome, she brought with her not just her baby son and her little brother-husband, Ptolemy XIV, she also brought architects and artisans familiar with the Egyptian style of monument building. Caesar quickly put them to work, reforming and rebuilding public structures all through the city. His building projects

had more than a hint of Egyptian influence, and it was clear to see the queen's influence on all that he did.

⚜

He built a temple beside the Forum and dedicated it to Venus Genetrix (Venus the Mother). In front of the temple he placed a huge statue of himself as the new Alexander the Great, and inside, next to the statue of the goddess, he erected a golden image of Cleopatra cradling their child in her arms. In Egypt, equating the kings with the gods was commonplace, but in Rome it was unheard-of. "That the honor had been given not to a Roman but to a foreigner and a woman caused shock, outrage and heightened speculation about Caesar's intentions toward the Egyptian queen."

⚜

Rome had reason to be concerned. Cleopatra had taken ambitions within her lover that he had long tried to conceal, and she had teased them out into the open. They planned to recreate the Empire of Alexander the Great, the queen's fabled ancestor, with themselves at the head. Clearly, Caesar had come to think of himself as a king, and he had every intention of living that way.

⚜

The Roman Senate was enormously hostile to the idea of royalty. Within living memory, the men of Rome had overthrown the dictator Sulla in favor of setting up a true Republic. Less than a generation had passed since the dictator's downfall, and the idea of another absolute ruler was unsettling. Worse still was the fact that this would-be king was

entirely under the influence of another, a foreign woman who was also an absolute monarch in her own right. Cleopatra's considerable influence over Julius Caesar was a source of constant concern, and as time went on, the proto-royal activities that Caesar pursued were blamed on her.

※

In truth, he was ambitious to a fault already. He was already well on his way to dictatorship when they met. It is disingenuous to accuse Cleopatra of being the cause of Caesar's imperial hopes, although it is safe to say that she encouraged their growth.

THE KING OF ROME

✿

In 46 BC, the sons of the late Pompey gathered men and arms and began to rebel against Caesar in the province of Spain. Sextus and Gaeus, Pompey's heirs, were a thorn in Caesar's side, and he had to do something about them. He left Rome abruptly with his army, embarking on the last campaign of his war with his old friend's family.

✿

THE BATTLE WAS WON by Caesar, although it was hard-fought and saw him dismounting and rushing into battle on foot to shame his own men into fighting harder. He slaughtered the rebels who had been taken captive, and with Antony at his side, he rode back home in yet another triumph.

✿

IT'S NOT KNOWN what Cleopatra did while her husband was

otherwise occupied in Spain. Some believe that she returned to Alexandria to ensure that her own reign was still secure. Others think that she stayed in the villa, awaiting her man's return. What is known is that by the time Caesar returned to his villa outside Rome, she was at his side once again.

❦

THE FIGHTING HAD BEEN PARTICULARLY HARD, and the strain had been so great that Caesar's old illness (epilepsy) suffered a flare-up that put him in mind of his mortality. He paused at his villa before returning to the city proper, possibly with Cleopatra beside him, and took the time to write his will.

❦

HIS VICTORY over the sons of Pompey signaled his destruction of the old Roman Republic. There was nothing left to prevent him from taking control of Rome as her sole master. In 44 BC, the Senate – presumably over the complaints and objections of Republicans like Cicero, Cassius and Brutus – proclaimed Caesar "dictator perpetuo," or dictator for life. In a public celebration, Antony offered Caesar a golden diadem, which he waved away three times, playing to the crowd and pretending to be the reluctant leader who was having royalty thrust upon him.

❦

CLEOPATRA and his enemies knew better. Caesar wanted to be king.

THE IDES OF MARCH

❦

In 44 BC, in the month of March, Caesar was feeling invulnerable. Over objections from both Cleopatra and Mark Antony, he dismissed his body guards and chose to go unprotected to the Senate. There had been firestorms of rumors regarding plots to kill the Roman dictator, and Cleopatra implored him to be cautious, but Caesar would have none of it. The Father of his Country did not believe his "children" would ever do him any harm.

❦

HE WAS WRONG.

❦

CAESAR HAD RECEIVED a warning from a soothsayer that he would not be safe until after the Ides of March (March 15th). Like most Romans, Caesar believed in prophesy, but he also

believed in his own immortality, especially now that he had been convinced of his divinity by the Living Isis, Cleopatra. On the morning of the 15th, believing that he had avoided his fate by reaching the day in one piece, he resolved to go to the Senate as usual. Again, Antony and Cleopatra pleaded with him not to go, but he would not be dissuaded. Antony went with him, intent upon keeping his friend safe.

᭰᭰᭰

AT THE SENATE, the conspirators had gathered, and they had planned their endeavor carefully. One of their number pulled Antony aside and prevented him from accompanying Caesar into the Senate while the rest of the crowd bore the dictator inside. Once there, the conspirators fell on Caesar with knives, and he was stabbed twenty-three times. His killers immediately fled, as did Antony, who had reason to believe that he was next. Cicero, who was a strong supporter of the plan even if he did not participate in it, loudly opined that Antony should have been killed, too.

᭰᭰᭰

CLEOPATRA AND CAESARION were in danger as well. Without Caesar to protect them, they were alone in a foreign land, with dangers and enemies on all sides. Working quickly, the queen gathered her child, her brother-husband, and their retinue and escaped to Alexandria as quickly as they could.

᭰᭰᭰

SHE MIGHT HAVE SUPPOSED that Caesar would have made provisions for his little son in his will, but Roman law prohibited bequests to any who were not Roman citizens. Instead,

he left everything, including the name of Caesar, to his nephew Octavius, who came to be known as Octavian. In a poignant footnote, every one of the men who took part in his murder were beneficiaries as well.

※

ANTONY EXPECTED to be named as Caesar's heir, and his surprise and hurt at being excluded were pushed aside as the necessary work of securing Rome continued. While Cleopatra fled home, civil war once again roared through Rome, with the "Liberators", as the assassins had begun to call themselves, on one side, and the newly-elected Triumvirate of Antony, Octavian and Lepidus on the other.

※

CLEOPATRA KNEW THAT OCTAVIAN, now named as Caesar's sole heir, would have every reason and every interest in eliminating her son. Caesarion had not been publicly claimed by the late Caesar, but he had also not been rejected. The little boy shared his illustrious father's name, and that was enough to be a death sentence if Octavian should ever get hold of him.

※

WITH CAESAR GONE and her world in turmoil, Cleopatra ordered the death of her brother. When Ptolemy XIV was strangled to death, she became the last and only queen of Egypt. Only Arsinoe still remained to contend for the throne, but she was still in Ephesus. Although she had suffered a great personal loss, and despite the loss of her greatest protector, Cleopatra had a secure

grasp on Egypt, which was the richest country in the world.

๑๛๑

SHE HAD Caesar's only son, and she had coffers filled with gold. It was only a matter of time before the Romans came for it all.

❦ V ❧

ANTONY AND CLEOPATRA

In praising Antony I have dispraised Caesar.
  Cleopatra

❦

In the ensuing chaos of war and retribution, all of the Liberators were either slain in battle or committed suicide to avoid the judgment and punishment that would have been handed down to them. Octavian and Antony put aside their personal strains to work together toward the common end of bringing their hero's killers to justice. The two men had never liked one another, and their personalities were nearly polar opposites. Their uneasy alliance fell apart not long after the last, decisive battle of the new civil war, the Battle of Philippi.

❦

With the fighting over, the new Triumvirate picked up the pieces that Caesar's death had scattered. Lepidus took control of the western part of the empire, like Gaul and Spain. Octavian took the city of Rome and the center of the continent of Europe, while Antony took control of the eastern provinces.

⚜

It was in this capacity that Antony marched east, gathering money and honors, repeating the old Alexandrine process of visiting and praying at every major temple along the way. He paid visits to all of the provincial rulers who had sided with Caesar's murderers in the brief civil war following the assassination, shaking them down for immense sums. He reached out to Cleopatra, sending a missive asking her – or ordering her, depending on interpretation – to come to see him in the city of Tarsus, which is in modern-day Turkey and was already ancient in those days. He enjoyed the privilege of being named 'the New Dionysus,' an honor that was bestowed upon him at the Temple of Artemis in Ephesus, where he encountered Arsinoe for the first time. He had long worshipped Dionysus, the god of wine, and the accolade suited him. It also gave him a reason to declare some divinity of his own.

⚜

He was proud and secure in his newfound power, but if he thought he would overawe Cleopatra, he was very much mistaken. The Queen of Egypt, in her full glory as the reincarnation of the goddess Isis, was coming to accept his invitation as only she could.

THE GODDESS OF LOVE

⚜

I t was a scene out of a movie, and another example of
Cleopatra's sense of theatricality. She made Antony wait
for her, keeping him in Tarsus cooling his heels until she
was ready to see him. If he had ever thought he could order
her, he was seeing the error of his ways. She prepared carefully, and when she finally arrived at their meeting place,
Cleopatra was the center of a spectacle that rivalled anything
Antony had ever seen.

⚜

THE QUEEN SAILED to Tarsus on her pleasure boat, a vessel
that was virtually a floating palace complete with gardens,
gilded and bedecked with artworks that hearkened back to
the tales of Hercules, from whom Antony's family claimed
descent. She sent word to the waiting Roman that "Aphrodite
was coming to revel with Dionysus for the good of Asia," and
she had herself dressed as Isis and Aphrodite conflated. The

ship flew purple sails and was propelled by silver oars, and clouds of perfume marked its passing. She sat on the deck beneath a canopy covered in stars, a goddess in her holy temple.

❧

ANTONY'S INVITATION had been to join him in the Forum of Tarsus. When she arrived, Cleopatra issued a counteroffer, inviting him to come and dine with her on her pleasure barge, his god to her goddess. Subtly, she was asserting control, and leaving it up to Antony to subject himself to her will, at least symbolically.

❧

HE ACCEPTED her invitation and joined her on her ship, where she showered him with gold and silver and priceless gifts. They discussed the recent war, and the troublesome matter of some Egyptian ships supporting his enemies in battle, and she convinced him that she had never betrayed his friendship. He and his officers were invited back for dinner the next night, and when they returned, their reception was even grander than before. The queen talked and charmed, and her ladies flirted with the soldiers, and before the end of the evening she issued another invitation for the following night, this time to host Antony alone.

❧

THE QUEEN SURPRISED Antony on that third day by suddenly accepting his invitation and coming ashore to see him in the Forum of Tarsus. He could not mount a reception anywhere as grand as what she had given him, and he even joked about

with her in self-effacing embarrassment. Graciously, Cleopatra assured him that he was the perfect host, simply presenting the true face of who he really was. His pride was salvaged, and her flattery was well received.

❧

ON THE THIRD NIGHT, Antony and Cleopatra dined in private aboard her sumptuous ship, and whatever they discussed is not recorded. She must have worked the same magic she had done with Caesar, though, because by morning, Antony had ordered the murder of Arsinoe in Ephesus, removing the last possible threat to Cleopatra's rule.

❧

IT WAS the queen's glamorous version of shock and awe, and it had worked like a dream. From that third dinner to the end of their lives, Antony was, quite simply, hers. After their night together, Cleopatra made ready to return to Alexandria, and she invited Antony to accompany her there. There was never any doubt what his answer was going to be.

❧ VI ❧

AN ALEXANDRIAN IDYLL

Be it known that we, the greatest, are misthought.
Cleopatra

❧

Antony was distracted by the business of empire and was delayed in joining Cleopatra in Alexandria, but she made good use of the time. She had studied the man, and having known him as one of Caesar's friends, she had an excellent understanding of what made Antony tick. She was preternaturally talented at reading and manipulating people, a consummate actress and political animal whose talent for molding men to her whims was matched only by her ambition. She was always the one holding the power, and she intended for it to stay that way.

❧

When Antony finally sailed to Alexandria in 41 BC, Cleopatra met him with another extravagant welcome, this one even larger and grander than the one on her barge. She had made certain to appeal to each of Antony's vices and some of his virtues, and he was utterly besotted.

⚜

Unlike other Roman generals and men of power before him, he did not arrive with legions and lictors, and none of the trappings of his consulship accompanied him to Alexandria. Instead he dressed like a Greek civilian and spent his days exploring the city, walking the streets and pretending to be a normal, ordinary citizen.

⚜

Everywhere he went, Cleopatra was at his side. She rarely let him out of her sight. She accompanied him on hunts in the Delta, to games of chance, and to licentious parties thrown by members of the Society of Inimitable Livers. This group was a bacchanalian outfit that she had created for Antony from the cream of Alexandria's Macedonian society. Antony's patron god was Bacchus, so it was a calculated construction. The two of them spent many hours, and their hosts spent exorbitant sums, enjoying drink, music, and theater.

⚜

Antony was not entirely given to leisure, although that was the word that was sent back to Rome. He trained hard, as well, working side by side with his soldiers as was his wont, something that had earned him their devotion. While Cicero and Octavian eviscerated his character in Rome by declaring

him dissolute and unduly influenced by the Egyptian queen, he exercised and maintained his fighting form, all the while closely watched and admired by Cleopatra.

❧

The queen was fully committed to seducing him, utterly and completely. As Diana Preston writes,

> "Cleopatra intended to be everything to Antony – to fill his days and satisfy his nights to the exclusion of all else."

This was more than the expression of a woman's lust for a handsome and virile man, however; she was shrewd in all things, and she needed to convince Antony to bind himself to her, to protect her and her country. Everything Cleopatra did, ultimately, was for the good of Egypt.

❧

That is not to say that her feelings for Antony were insincere. Quite the contrary, the two were devoted and adored one another. They were similar in many ways, not least in their natural inclinations toward excess, their naked ambition, and their prodigious physical appetites. They were exceedingly well matched, and they would become each other's world.

❧

It was during their first winter together that Cleopatra again became pregnant. She hoped that the baby would make Antony stay, but like Caesar before him, he sailed out in the spring, headed for war. He was embarking on a campaign

against the Parthians, who had invaded Rome's holdings in Judea, and though he might have wanted to stay in Cleopatra's pleasure palace, he had to answer the call of the other half of his nature. He was a lover, certainly, but Antony was first and foremost a fighter.

BAD NEWS AND UNHELPFUL
RELATIVES

๑๕๕

W hen Antony left Alexandria, he went to Tyre, where he found that several vassal kings had defected to the Parthians, and that many of his troops in Syria had deserted. Worse, he learned that his brother, Lucius Antonius, and his deserted wife, Fulvia, were causing trouble back in Rome. They were antagonizing Octavian and spreading scandalous rumors about the price he had paid for his inheritance from Caesar. Roman society was once again splintering. Meanwhile, Sextus Pompey, the last surviving child of Pompey the Great, who had begun to run a pirating operation out of Sicily, preying on Roman ships. It was chaos.

๑๕๕

LUCIUS AND FULVIA instigated an armed insurrection aimed at forcing Octavian to relinquish his part of the Triumvirate to Antony. Their failure was epic, but their target was far too

politically astute to kill them, knowing that Antony still had supporters in Rome, and that any such action would bring sympathy to his rival's side. Lucius was made governor of Spain, where he died not long after of dubiously natural causes, and Fulvia and her sons with Antony were allowed to escape to Greece.

࿇

ANTONY WAS INCENSED WITH FULVIA, and the crisis at home was such that he was obliged to abandon his Parthian campaign. He met up with Fulvia in Greece, and he accused her of causing trouble to wrest him from Cleopatra's side. She did not deny it. He left her and their children in Greece and tried to patch things up with Octavian, whom he despised but needed. Fulvia was ill and depressed, and she died not long after Antony's departure, possibly by her own hand.

࿇

THE DAMAGE HAD ALREADY BEEN DONE. Thanks to the inept meddling of Fulvia and Lucius, Octavian had marched on Antony, who was busy besieging the city of Brundisium in an attempt to make his abandoned Parthian campaign a reality. Octavian caught Antony between a Roman army and the walls of the besieged city, and Antony was forced to accept humiliating terms that included the loss of his lands in Gaul and his agreement to honor Octavian by marrying his sister, Octavia.

THE SUN AND THE MOON

❦

I n Alexandria, Cleopatra could only watch and wait as Roman politics unraveled and her personal life frayed along with it. She gave birth to twins, Alexander Helios and Cleopatra Selene. The news reached Rome at about the same time as Antony's arranged marriage to Octavia, a match that brought him closer to Octavian, who was Cleopatra's mortal enemy. She knew, beyond a shadow of a doubt, that Octavian was a threat to her firstborn son, and now her lover was making alliances with him. The situation was not at all to her liking.

❦

TO MAKE MATTERS WORSE, the Parthians were taking advantage of the distractions in Rome and were marching Rome's eastern territories. This brought them to within striking distance of Cleopatra's own borders. Unable to protect his lover himself, Antony sent one of his generals to

keep the Parthians away from Egypt, which he did with great aplomb and glorification. That glory should have been Antony's, had he not been bogged down with his new, constricted life.

⊗

HE WAS KEPT AWAY from Cleopatra for three and a half years. She raised her children on her own, teaching them in the Ptolemaic fashion to be Greek scholars and Egyptian god-kings. She and Antony exchanged letters, and she continually exhorted him not to trust Octavian, as if that was ever really an option.

⊗

THE ROMAN WAGS and Senatorial grumbling classes loved Octavia almost as much as they loathed Cleopatra. The Roman matron was the ideal patrician partner for Antony, keeping him from his worst excesses and forcing him to mind his domestic (i.e., Roman) responsibilities instead of engaging in feasts and follies with his lover in Alexandria. She bore him two daughters, and while he still entertained his friends and drank too much, he was more sedate and "proper" in his ways than he had been when he had been with Cleopatra. The Senate and Octavian were mollified, and it seemed that Antony had at last been tamed.

⊗

WHILE OUTRIGHT WAR WAS AVOIDED, Octavian and Antony sniped and snarled at one another in propaganda and in the court of public opinion. Always, Octavian came out on top in their war of words. He was a much craftier statesman than

Antony, who had always been at heart a rough soldier. By way of an astrologer that she had hired and who was attached to Antony's household, presumably to report back to the queen and to express her wishes to her lover, Cleopatra urged Antony to put more physical distance between himself and his fellow triumvir, and Antony complied. Octavian, though, continually called him back, then humiliated him by refusing to meet with him, presenting instead a number of contrived excuses. Octavia became pregnant again, and the pressure of mounting personal discontent drove Antony to once more prepare to fight the Parthians.

HE SENT his family back to Rome and proceeded to Antioch, the capital of Syria. Once he was free of his wife and in-laws, he sent for Cleopatra, and she happily met him there, bringing the twins with her to meet their father for the first time. Antony had coins struck to celebrate their reunion, with his head on one side and Cleopatra's head on the other. He never laid eyes on his Roman wife again.

❧ VII ❧

DUSK APPROACHES

Is he a good man?" "Define 'good'.
  Cleopatra

❧

In Antioch, Antony presented Cleopatra with a host of honors and new lands as gifts. His actions infuriated his brother-in-law, who feigned great wrath at the insult to his sister, Octavia. The territories that he presented to Cleopatra belonged to Rome, and were not his to give away. His detractors in the Senate and in Rome's aristocracy accused him of falling prey to mindless sensuality and a complete loss of self-control, and that he had become unmanned by Cleopatra. This was an angry and hateful spin on the political intelligence of the gifts, however; each of these territories was on the border of Egypt, and they increased a buffer zone between the queen and the increasingly hostile Octavian.

꧁꧂

After a few months of enjoying their renewed affair, the couple separated once again. Cleopatra, who had just become pregnant with another of Antony's children, returned to Alexandria while Antony turned his attention to the long-delayed Parthian campaign. He met with defeat, an uncommon occurrence for him, for he had always been a talented soldier and leader. His failure was due in no small part to the defection and betrayal of his army by his supposed ally, the king of Armenia, Artavasdes. The Armenian gave up the Roman positions and battle plans to the Parthians, and the results were calamitous. By the end of the campaign, Roman legionaries were starving and deserted, and Antony himself contemplated suicide.

꧁꧂

He managed to rally out of his depression and led his men on a retreat back to Roman lands, where he sent for Cleopatra, asking her to come and resupply his suffering troops. He was despondent while he awaited her arrival, unaccustomed to military failure. His embarrassment was compounded by news of Octavian's successes against Sextus Pompey, whose pirates were finally destroyed, and against Lepidus, whose ill-advised rebellion Octavian smashed. Lepidus was expelled from the Triumvirate, leaving only Octavian and Antony as the leaders of Rome. Everyone knew that Octavian intended to remove Antony, as well.

꧁꧂

Antony was normally well-loved by his men, but the Octavian and Ciceronian propaganda machine turned against him.

Cleopatra was solidly blamed for the Parthian defeat, despite the fact that it had been Armenia's betrayal that doomed the campaign. Antony's personal life was a subject of ridicule, as the abandoned Octavia played the part of the perfect Roman matron, eliciting pity for herself and her children and heaps of scorn for Antony.

⚜

Antony was not one to take defeat lying down. He wintered in Alexandria with his beloved queen and their young family, but his mind was on war. When spring came, he returned to the field with his legions, intent upon avenging himself upon the treacherous Armenian king. This time, he returned in triumph, dragging Atravasdes along in chains.

⚜

His military success would have gained Antony some much-needed support in Rome, but he erred badly, and perhaps fatally. Instead of going back to Rome and enriching the coffers of the state, he returned instead to Alexandria, where he presented the spoils of war and the imprisoned king to Cleopatra. His triumph was capped by a public ceremony where he and Cleopatra sat together on golden thrones, and he declared her "the Queen of Queens" and Caesarion, her heir and now co-ruler, as "King of Kings".

⚜

Rome exploded in spite and fury. Antony claimed that he was acting only to ensure Julius Caesar's wishes for his widow and child, but this was obviously untrue, and one of the clumsiest lies of his political career. In retaliation, Octavian seized

Antony's will, which had been sealed and stored in a temple in Rome, and had it read aloud. In it, Antony bequeathed everything he owned – including much Roman territory – to his Egyptian queen and their progeny.

❧

Octavian finally had license to do what he had always wanted. He condemned Antony and Cleopatra enemies of the state, and he declared war upon them both.

❧

It is important to note that Octavian never declared war on Egypt – rather, he aimed his bellicose rage at the person of Cleopatra, the woman whose son and whose influence were the only true barriers between himself and sole domination of Rome. He had already envisioned becoming the first emperor or Rome, but he could not do this for so long as his strength and support came only because of his position as Caesar's heir. He could not allow his uncle's true heir, his only son, Ceasarion, to continue to exist as a shadow at his back. He began to obsess about Cleopatra and Antony, desperate to claim the queen as a trophy of war that he could abase in the Roman Forum. He knew that this would never happen for as long as Antony was alive.

❧

The die was cast.

THE BEGINNING OF THE END

෨෨

C leopatra was obviously not willing to be anyone's trophy, and she was a dedicated and devoted mother who would do anything it took to ensure the survival of her children and the welfare of the Egyptian people. For all of her Roman complications, she was a beloved and loyal queen who treated her subjects with fairness and an open hand. She lived for Egypt, and for her children, and for Antony.

෨෨

THE TWO OF them devoted themselves entirely to one another after the declaration of war. The famously philandering Antony became a one-woman man and never took another lover. He declared Cleopatra his wife and named his children as his heirs, no longer trying to bow to the politics of Rome. His oldest son, Antyllus, joined him in Alexandria. The Egyptian army and navy were strong, and combined with

the legions who still gave their loyalty to Antony, they were a formidable force.

⚜

CLEOPATRA AND ANTONY knew that Octavian was coming, and that he would bring the weight of Rome with him. They reached out to their neighbors in the near east, but their efforts at alliance were rebuffed as kingdom after kingdom saw the writing on the wall and threw in with Rome.

⚜

CLEOPATRA AND ANTONY were not fools. They knew that Rome was too mighty an enemy to be defeated, and that their chances of emerging from this conflict were poor. Antony's generals disliked Cleopatra. She sat at Antony's side as his equal, a complete violation of Roman gender politics. She gave them orders and expected them to be obeyed, and foreigners were always to be subservient to their Roman masters. Cleopatra was too proud, they said, too aggressive. They accused her of duplicity and ambition for the destruction of Rome, beginning with the destruction of Antony. His friends turned from him.

⚜

HE WAS TOLD that all would be forgiven if he simply killed Cleopatra and took the kingdom of Egypt for Rome. The thought was anathema to him, and he refused. Antony resolved to defend his wife and children, and Cleopatra levied new taxes to raise funds to support his war effort. She also began work on a splendid tomb in Alexandria, a "House of Eternity" where she and Antony could be laid to rest

68

together. As a true Egyptian pharaoh, she was concerned about her place in the afterlife, and building an elaborate tomb long before the first hint of approaching death was an Egyptian royal tradition. To Antony's soldiers, though, it looked dire and pessimistic, and they believed that Cleopatra had no faith in them and was preparing to lose. It was a morale breaker, something that Cleopatra never understood. The Roman soldiers, feeling unsupported by their own leaders, deserted to Octavian's camp.

❧

OCTAVIAN BLOCKADED EGYPT, and he sent messages to Antony advising that he had declared war on Cleopatra alone, beckoning Antony to return to the fold. Meanwhile, he sent troops by land through the territories of his new friends, intending to attack Egypt from the east and Judea, whose Roman puppet leader Herod was a devoted enemy of the Egyptian queen. After illness swept through his army, and after a series of desertions, Antony was badly outnumbered on the land. Cleopatra urged him to break Octavian's blockade, both to alleviate the suffering of the Egyptian people and to win a victory that might turn opinion back to his side. Reluctantly, he agreed.

❧

THE END CAME at the Battle of Actium. It was not the last battle of the war, but it was the worst defeat. Antony and Cleopatra sailed out to meet Octavian in the Mediterranean near the city of Actium, he on his battle ship amid his Roman quadriremes, she on the Egyptian flagship in the midst of her fleet. They faced Octavian, who brought the entire Roman navy, but most importantly, he put that navy under the

command of the foremost genius of the day, the admiral Agrippa.

⚜

IT WAS A ROUT. Antony's ships were set aflame by burning missiles from Octavian's side, and when he signaled for Cleopatra to bring her ships in to relieve and assist him, she instead withdrew and took her fleet back to the safety of Alexandria, leaving Antony behind. Her flight was portrayed as betrayal and cowardice, but in truth, it may have been intended all along. Antony would have wanted his wife and children safe, and the only way that would happen would be for Cleopatra to return to Egypt. The signal that was taken as a plea for aid may well have been an order to retreat. In any case, Antony turned his ship and followed her as well, fleeing from the battle and abandoning his men to the tender mercies of Octavian.

⚜

ANTONY WAS INCONSOLABLE. He spent three days alone, sitting in the prow of his warship with his head in his hands. When he finally bestirred himself, he gathered his few remaining supporters and tried to give away all of his possessions, which they tearfully declined. He promised to negotiate their safe return to Rome when Octavian came, and in shame, he went traveling to his allies in North Africa, begging for reinforcements. None would come. In Cyrene, he attempted suicide, but two loyal friends still with him stayed his hand and urged him to return to Alexandria.

⚜

THINGS in the Egyptian capital were not going any better. The Macedonian aristocracy, smelling blood, abandoned Cleopatra en masse. They would not support her or any of her attempts to bolster the city in preparation for Octavian's inevitable arrival. In fact, despite the many honors and favors they had received from the queen and from Antony during the happy years, they made it clear that they intended to deliver the city and her queen into the Roman conqueror's outstretched hands.

৯৬৯

WITH NO HOPE for the future remaining, Cleopatra distracted Antony from his despair as well as she could. His brush with suicide had chilled her, and she did everything she could to keep him happy. She threw parties for him and their dwindling circle of friends, and then capped it off with an elaborate joint coming-of-age celebration for Caesarion, who was 16 years old, and Antony's oldest son, Antyllus, who was 15. It was a last declaration of defiance to Octavian, displaying that there was still a future in Egypt, where there were two healthy sons, while Octavian himself was the father of just one sickly girl.

৯৬৯

THROUGH ALL OF the partying and the desperate flailing attempts to emulate happiness, Cleopatra sent letter after letter to Octavian. She begged him to allow her to abdicate in favor of her children, to continue the Ptolemaic line in subservience to Rome. Her offer was rebuffed; Octavian had no intention of allowing another Ptolemy to rise to power. Antony sent a letter to Octavian offering to surrender in return for living out his life as a private citizen in Alexandria,

or in Athens. Octavian never bothered to respond, ignoring Antony completely. His response to Cleopatra's overtures was to publicly threaten her, and to privately tell her that she could gain clemency only by murdering Antony. As Antony had refused to kill her, she now refused to harm him, and by their loyalty to one another, they sealed their fates.

༺❦༻

OCTAVIAN MADE one last overture to Cleopatra. He sent a handsome soldier named Thyrsus to the queen as his emissary, bringing letters alleging Octavian's infatuation with her, which was as bizarre as it was false. Thyrsus was specially selected for his job because he was intelligent, like Caesar, and brutally handsome, like Antony; he had virile charm and vigor, and Cleopatra received him warmly. She met with him in private, probably to attempt to negotiate a better end for herself and for her children, but Antony misunderstood. He exploded with jealous rage and had Thyrsus apprehended, beaten, and returned to Octavian with an angry letter. To hedge his bets, he also sent Antyllus with gifts of gold. Octavian ignored the letter, dismissed Thyrsus and Antyllus, and continued his inexorable approach.

❧ VIII ❧

SUNSET

Leave the fishing-rod, Great General, to us sovereigns of Pharos and Canopus. Your game is cities and kings and continents.

Cleopatra

❦

In her youth, Cleopatra had studied medicine and poisons. She now resumed those studies with her royal physician at her side, searching for a venom that was both as lethal and as painless as possible. She celebrated her thirty-eighth birthday with a subdued party, and Antony's fifty-third year was greeted in the same way. The Society of Inimitable Livers, the club the couple had formed with their party friends, was disbanded and renamed "Companions to the Death". Work on the mausoleum was intensified.

❦

Cleopatra received more lying missives from Octavian, urging her to kill Antony and to take himself as her lover, for he professed great desire for her. She knew that his infatuation was not with her, but with the great wealth in Egypt. She made it known to Octavian that if she were to disappear, that wealth would disappear as well. The approaching Roman was horrified by the thought, and his reaction made it clear where his heart truly lay.

❦

In July, 30 BC, Octavian at last reached Alexandria. His army encamped outside the city limits, visible from the heights of the palace. Antony and Cleopatra had one last mournful celebration with their last faithful friends, at which time Antony told his men that in the morning they would have a new master, and he would be "a mummy or a nothing." His men wept to hear his anticipation of defeat, but none could disagree with his prediction.

❦

On August 1, 30 BC, Antony led his chariots out to meet Octavian in one last battle. Cleopatra barricaded herself in her mausoleum with her two maidservants and sent word to Antony that she was dead. Perhaps she thought he would fight harder if he thought he was fighting in her memory. Perhaps she hoped that by seeming to be removed from his life, she could inspire him to save himself.

❦

Her message did the opposite. On receiving the news of her supposed demise, Antony turned to his trusted slave, Eros, and ordered him to take his life. Eros drew his sword, but slew himself instead, falling at Antony's feet in one last display of adoration. Antony then drew his sword and stabbed himself, but he bungled the act and missed his heart, succeeding only in self-evisceration. He asked the soldiers around him to help him and complete the job, but they abandoned him instead, leaving him dying and deserted.

❧

He was brought to the mausoleum, bleeding and in agony, where he was taken to Cleopatra. His reaction at learning that she still lived is not recorded, but it is known that he drew his last breath while lying in her arms. Cleopatra went mad with grief, tearing at her hair and smearing herself with her husband's blood. Almost immediately, an emissary from Octavian arrived to offer her clemency if she would only deliver herself to the enemy camp. She knew that the offer was a lie.

❧

She gathered herself and her pride. She was a queen, and she would not end her glorious life being strangled in the Forum. Cleopatra bathed and dressed herself in her royal regalia, her beauty shining as fully as it ever had. She locked herself into the mausoleum with two maidservants and the corpse of her beloved Antony, and there, in a final act that has echoed through the centuries, she committed suicide by enticing a venomous snake to bite her on the breast.

❧

Cleopatra was dead. The pharaohs of Egypt were no more.

❧ IX ❧
REQUIEM FOR A QUEEN

And make death proud to take us.
    Cleopatra

❧❧❧

In the end, Cleopatra stole one last victory from Octavian, denying him the triumph he so desperately wanted. Both Antony and Cleopatra had prevented him from the glory of seeing his enemies humiliated in the Forum, and his rage was epic. He had Caesarion murdered immediately, then returned to Rome, enriched by the gold of Egypt but forever prevented from the one thing that would have given him happiness. He went on to become the first Emperor of Rome, renaming himself Caesar Augustus.

❧❧❧

His apologists and supporters slandered Cleopatra both during her life and after her death as a monster, a woman who did not know her womanly place. They hated her for her ambition, and for daring to think herself the equal of any man. They painted her as little better than a whore, selling herself to any man who could grant her the power she so desperately craved.

৩৯৫৩

Their words distorted the image of the queen that has come down to us. The true Cleopatra was very different.

৩৯৫৩

She was a brilliant woman, intelligent and well educated. She enticed and bewitched two of the most powerful men in Rome not just through her beauty, which was considerable, but through her skill and acumen, her wisdom and her intellect. She dared to think herself their equal because that's exactly what she was.

৩৯৫৩

Cleopatra was the last pharaoh of Egypt, and unlike her Macedonian forebears, she loved her country and its ancient ways. She brought the cult of Isis and the ancient faith of Egypt back to vibrant life, and she built monuments and public works that improved the lives of common Egyptians. If she sometimes slighted the Macedonian elite in Alexandria, it was because she had turned her heart and her will toward the betterment of the common people of Egypt, who had always supported her.

❧❦❧

Her reputation for sexual excess is belied by the fact that she only had two lovers in her life, and both she considered her husbands: Julius Caesar and Mark Antony. If soulmates exist, then Antony was hers, and she was his. Their bitter romance has survived not just because of its tragic ending, but because of it depth and abiding power. She lived for Egypt and for Antony, and she died for them as well.

❧❦❧

When history books portray Cleopatra as a grasping fiend with more ambition than sense, remember that the truth is not necessarily what the stories say. She was more than her Roman detractors would have us believe.

❧ X ❧
FOR ADDITIONAL
READING

❧

Cleopatra: A Life, Stacy Schiff, © 2010, Little, Brown and Company, New York, New York.

❧

Cleopatra: A Sourcebook, Prudence Jones, editor, © 2006, University of Oklahoma Press, Tulsa, Oklahoma.

❧

Cleopatra and Antony: Power, Love and Politics in the Ancient World, Diane Preston, © 2009 Walker Publishing Company, New York, New York.

❧

Cleopatra the Great: The Woman Behind the Legend, Dr. Joann Fletcher, © 2011 Harper Collins, New York, New York.

࿐

The Divine Julius Caesar, Plutarch, translated by Prudence Jones, © 2006, University of Oklahoma Press, Tulsa, Oklahoma.

࿐

Egypt in the Age of Cleopatra, Michael Chauveau, translated by David Lorton, © 2000 Cornell University Press, New York, New York.

࿐

Life of Antony, Plutarch, translated by Prudence Jones, © 2006, University of Oklahoma Press, Tulsa, Oklahoma.

YOUR FREE EBOOK!

As a way of saying thank you for reading our book, we're offering you a free copy of the below eBook.

Happy Reading!

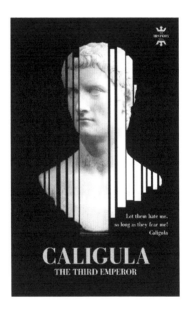

90450022R00054

Made in the USA
Middletown, DE
23 September 2018

CLEOPATRA

THE EGYPTIAN QUEEN

THE HISTORY HOUR